AND
SURRENDER FEAR

by
Mark Thurston, Ph.D.

A·R·E PRESS

ASSOCIATION FOR
RESEARCH AND
ENLIGHTENMENT

A.R.E. Press ● Virginia Beach ● Virginia

CONTENTS

. . . until ye are willing to lose thyself in service, ye may not indeed know that peace which He has promised to give—to all.

Edgar Cayce reading 1599-1

Introduction

Peace is probably the most elusive quality of life. For a fleeting moment on a hectic day, you may find the time to relax. Then it's back to all your demanding responsibilities. Or for a few days you might get away from the noisy bustle of modern living and discover a little peace and quiet. But all too soon, the tranquility evaporates as you have to return to the real world.

Our needs for peace reach inward, too. Worries, doubts, and fears destroy peace of mind and heart. Just when we think we've found inner stability, something comes along to throw us off balance.

Of the thousands of people who came to Edgar Cayce for advice, most were looking for peace. They may not have always posed their questions in those terms. But their troubled souls and wounded bodies were calling out for something that would bring them peace.

Edgar Cayce is America's best-documented clairvoyant and spiritual philosopher. Over a period of forty-three years during the first half of the twentieth century, he gave over 14,000 psychic discourses for distressed people. This material addresses all the basic themes of human experience—none more important than how to find peace in the modern world.

His approach to peace was clearly a spiritual one. The philosophy of life found in these readings points to an invisible realm of the spirit as the place where all peace begins. From that basic assumption, two ideas are right at the heart of his message about peace.

First, *everything is trying to move to-*

ward peace. As he put it in his reading for one woman, "The whole of God's creation seeks harmony and peace!" (1742-4) Of course, that isn't always obvious when we look at life from our own, limited perspective. A lot of what goes on seems anything but an impulse toward greater peace. But maybe we need to learn how to see more deeply the motives and purposes that guide human affairs. Perhaps, as an undercurrent to everything, we'd discover the desire for peace.

Second, Cayce offers us a hopeful idea: *God has promised peace to each of us*. In fact, promises were something that came up time and again when Cayce counseled people about their troubled, painful, fearful lives. "Peace . . . is the greater promise that has ever been made to man" (543-11), Cayce told one individual. Peace is promised to us. Of course, it takes some effort on our part to claim that assurance. We've got to hold up our end of the bargain. We've got to be willing to put aside our worries and our fears, allowing room for the peace that was pledged to us.

Claiming the promise is what this little book is all about. One by one, it addresses the ideas and the methods to get rid of fear and to find peace of mind and heart. Each small section of this guidebook focuses on a single principle, a spiritual truth that can help you discover a new way of moving through your day.

Take your time going through this volume. Spend a day—or sometimes several days—thinking about and applying a new way of looking at peace. Try out the ideas. Find the ones that work for you. That simple formula will get the best results.

Each section begins with a brief quote taken from one of the Cayce readings. (The numeric notation after each short passage indicates an indexing number within the collection of his work.) His messages are every bit as relevant, timely, and applicable today as they were when he gave them.

Following each of the short quotes is a commentary. Some of the commentaries elaborate on Cayce's central idea, but most of them tell the story of the person who received that advice from Cayce. (Fictitious names are used to preserve anonymity.) All these commentaries are designed to inspire you and to suggest ways to experience a fear-free, peaceful life.

Finally, each small section of this book concludes with a clear statement of how you could apply that principle. Each "minimotivator" is designed to get you focused and moving toward an *application* of some life-changing principle. It's by *acting* on these ideas that you're going to get results.

So let's get started. Only two things are required of you as we begin. First, you need to have recognized your own *sincere desire* to change the quality of how you're living your life. Second, you should feel a *willingness to experiment* with some changes. The results you'll get from this small book may surprise you.

Birthright

Only in casting thyself wholly upon the Lord may ye know the spiritual and mental peace that is the birthright of every soul. Only in defying same . . . ye become entangled in confusion, doubt and fear.

1326-1

What belongs to you from birth? What advantages are inherently yours—not political privileges, but spiritual rights? What experiences are yours for the asking, simply because you're a creation of God?

Peace is one of them. It's the birthright of every soul to have peace. Why, then, do so many throw away this privilege? In thousands of little ways people all over the world have chosen to defy this right. They have unwittingly given up the spiritual advantage that would transform the troubles of physical life.

Maybe the gift of peace is too hard for us to accept. If we think it's something we're supposed to earn — like other rewards that come from our accomplishments — then we probably don't feel worthy. Knowing that we haven't always acted very peacefully ourselves, we don't feel as if we deserve much peace in return.

But spiritual law doesn't always follow conventional wisdom. Sometimes the rules that God has set up for us don't follow the logic we'd expect. Whether we deserve it or not, some things are ours simply by wanting them. That's what a birthright means. And inner peace is at the top of the list.

Sylvia had lost touch with this principle. When she contacted Edgar Cayce for advice, she was in a state of despair. After three-and-a-half years of a troubled marriage, she and Jacob had separated. Now just a few weeks after he had left, she discovered she was pregnant with his child. She wanted Cayce's spiritual counsel: Should she attempt to win her husband back, and if so, how?

You don't have to win back anything, was the advice. The marriage may, in fact, be worth redeeming. But be careful in your approach. The harmony that you want isn't locked up inside your estranged husband. Peace is already yours. It's your birthright. Don't get caught in a game that you think you can win or lose.

How often do you remember that principle when you're troubled? How often do you think someone else holds the key to your own state of peace or turmoil? Instead, you can claim what's rightfully yours. Peace is already yours, just for the asking. It's not a question of deserving it, earning it, or winning it back. It's your birthright.

Mini-motivator: Simply claim peace for yourself today: peaceful thoughts, peaceful feelings, and a peaceful way of going about your duties. It belongs to you. No one can take it away from you. Keep that spiritual law in mind.

Inspiration

> . . . no emergency in a material way or manner may arise that may not find its counterpart in a spiritual inspiration.
>
> 877-7

Roger was at the top of his profession. As a corporate lawyer in New York City, he had made it big. At the age of forty-four he was co-owner of a seat on the New York Stock Exchange and was the envy of many. He had a solid marriage, reliable friends — and since having met Edgar Cayce several years earlier, he also had a meaningful spiritual direction for his life.

But in the spring of 1936, Roger was caught in fear. He had made a momentous decision to sell both his expensive waterfront home and his share of the brokerage firm. He was ready for something different; he felt that his soul *had to have* a change. He wasn't exactly sure what was next for him, but he had some ideas. Maybe teaching and writing. Perhaps trying to help other people more directly by working as a counselor.

But before anything like that could be explored, he had to find buyers for his large assets. He needed that money to sustain his family while he found his new way in the months ahead. Of course, it might not be easy in the economic hard times of the mid-1930s. So he began to grow afraid. Rather than be hopeful and excited about his recent prospects, he was beginning to let fear control his thinking. What if he couldn't find purchasers? What if he was simply deluding himself about being ready for another career?

The fear and doubt were becoming so strong that he turned to Cayce for advice. Words of encouragement came in that reading: an invitation to surrender his fears and be open to a calming inspiration. Hold fast to the sense of life purpose that you've been feeling from your inner self,

Cayce told him. Expect that people will offend you and that situations won't always seem to be going your way during this transition. But when doubt creeps in, remember that for every crisis or physical emergency, there is a counterbalancing inspiration. It will lift your spirits and quiet your troubled mind. To help you keep in touch with that possibility—to help you surrender your fears—use this visualization method: Imagine Jesus on the turbulent sea with His disciples and how He calmed the troubled waters.

When the typed transcript of the reading arrived at his home, it must have made a lot of sense to Roger. In a personal note back to Cayce that week he wrote: "The reading was perfect; I understand exactly what was meant, all the way through."

Something about this principle of inspiration rang true for him. Perhaps it does for us, too. No matter what kind of fearful emergency or anxious test we're facing, there's an antidote. Just as surely as modern physics teaches "for every action there's an equal and opposite reaction," so too does our inner life behave lawfully. In the depths of our anxiety and worry, something else is offered to us from the heights. When we're most seriously caught up in fear, that's when we have the best chance to feel the calming, strengthening power of God.

Mini-motivator: The next time a crisis or problem makes you fearful, pause and let the image of Christ calming the waters lift your spirits. Claim the promise that whenever you're at a low point, an inspiration is there waiting for you.

Avoiding Antagonism

Q-8. *Will the attacks come to naught that have been made on me by the American Medical Association?*

A-8. Depends upon the antagonistic attitude that the body assumes . . . If ye would have peace, be peaceful!   969-1

Peter was a man ahead of his times. Born in the last year of the Civil War, he had grown up to see his world change immeasurably. He had followed a career in medicine at a time when the modern field was just beginning to establish itself. In the early years of his profession, there was still considerable flexibility. New discoveries were occurring all the time. New therapies were competing for favor, and Peter open-mindedly embraced anything that offered help to his patients.

As his experience and skills expanded, he became a spokesman for several of the new methods, including chiropractic manipulation and iridology (diagnostic techniques using the iris of the eye). He wrote articles and lectured extensively about his medical beliefs. Some people admired his breadth of vision and openness. Others thought he was naive and gullible, risking his license as an M.D.

Conditions began to change for Peter as he neared the end of his career. By the 1930s what we now know as mainstream allopathic medicine had gained favor in America. There was little or no tolerance for alternative therapies. The American Medical Association was a powerful force trying to limit mavericks like Peter. He dreamed of opening a training institute in Washington, D.C.—a school of universal medicine. The A.M.A. bureaucrats dreamed of forcing Peter into retirement.

By the time he turned to Cayce for some advice, he was in hot water. An investigation was under way. The A.M.A. felt that it was simply trying to protect the public from an irresponsible doctor. He felt as if he were under attack from a close-minded organization that didn't really have his patients' best interests in mind. What was his proper line of defense? What kind of truce was possible so that peace could be re-established in his professional life?

Cayce's clairvoyant view of the problem described a remedy. It began with Peter's own attitude. Even though his words and behaviors were mild-mannered, inwardly he was agitated—even antagonistic. His mind was often filled with imagined arguments with A.M.A. officials. He was mentally plotting his next moves in the conflict.

Stop your belligerent attitude, Cayce advised. If you're mentally creating a showdown, you'll get one. By the law of attraction, antagonism in the outer world will come forth to meet your inner antagonism. But you can cut off the process. From your own mind you can stop feeding the growing battle. If you want peace, be peaceful—

especially in your thoughts.

Haven't we all faced struggles like Peter's? Maybe they haven't been so severe that our means of livelihood was in jeopardy. But upon careful reflection, we're likely to see that a similar process was at work. Our own antagonistic thoughts and feelings kept reinforcing the fight. Thus, our inner hostility was met by an outer one. We can only speculate whether the situation might have turned out differently if we hadn't broken the self-perpetuating sequence.

Mini-motivator: The next time you sense an impending conflict, do your part to stop the process cold. Refuse to be pulled into the friction. Cut off your thoughts of attack. Give peace a chance by being peaceful inwardly.

Casting Out Fear

Reduce this fear in the body by the meditation and prayer. Begin especially with those portions of the scripture that refer to promises to the individual that there is within self that which casts out fear . . .   4072-1

Robert felt hopelessly out of place in his world. All of his friends were overseas serving in the military in World War II, and he was at home with a strange ailment that disqualified him, an illness that also kept him from being very productive with his tremendous talents as an artist. Life seemed bleak to this twenty-six-year-old man.

His unusual physical problem began when he was twelve: an episode of severe muscle spasms. The family doctor thought it was simply the result of something he had eaten, but five years later the condition began recurring frequently, this time in a more serious form. Now the spasms led to fainting spells and brief comas.

The family consulted many specialists, but with no success. He was hospitalized and X-rayed from head to toe. He was tested for allergies. But every report came back with the same conclusion: he seemed to be perfectly fit. Even the physicians at the Mayo Clinic concluded that there was nothing they could do for him because they couldn't determine the cause of these spells. Robert and his family were up against a blank wall.

As a last resort they agreed to try the suggestion of Robert's cousin. She had read about Edgar Cayce in an article published by *Coronet* magazine. In their letter requesting a reading, only a single question was posed: What causes his fainting spells or comas?

As he had on thousands of other occasions, Cayce offered a clairvoyant diagnosis from hundreds of miles away. He saw

that at a physical level the condition came
from poor eliminations. Congestions in the
bowel were triggering reactions in the ner-
vous and endocrine systems. Treatments
were recommended: castor oil packs, mas-
sage, and dietary changes.

But then Cayce addressed the deeper
issue: What was the cause of those imbal-
ances in his eliminations? *Fear* played a
major role. If Robert wanted to experience
a total healing, it would mean overcoming
his fears. For him, one of the best ways to
do this would be through meditating on
specific portions of the Bible. The 14th
through 17th chapters of the Gospel of
John were particularly recommended. Here
Robert would find promises. In these pas-
sages we *all* can find spiritual reassurance
to begin to conquer our fears.

Mini-motivator: Take about ten minutes for each of four consecutive days to
try Cayce's remedy for fear. Each of those

days read one of the four chapters from John. At the end of your reading time, take a few more minutes to think about the verses in that chapter that were most meaningful to you.

Meditative Peace

Learn that quiet first within self, from within . . . wherein there may be the peace . . .   694-2

Meditation is like an oasis of peace in the midst of hectic schedules and worrisome responsibilities. In those ten or twenty minutes of daily quiet, it's possible to keep yourself centered and tranquil.

But anyone who has tried to keep a regular meditation discipline knows that it doesn't always work quite as well as expected. There are days when you may get up from your meditation session and feel no more peaceful than you did when you sat down. What's gone wrong on days like that?

The trouble is most likely the *approach*—the very attitude with which you tried to meditate. If you've carried with you into meditation the familiar mind-set of daily life, then the results from your meditation will probably be frustrating. If you've tried to transplant into your session your competitive, acquisitive approach to life, you will have discovered that it doesn't work for meditation.

What is this familiar approach to life that is so ill-suited for meditation? Throughout most of our waking hours we're striving—even straining—to reach goals and accomplish tasks. We're attempting to acquire things, like physical possessions or people's approval. Often, our efforts are tinged with competition as we try to prove ourselves. Simply put, we're trying to *get* something.

But what happens if you attempt to carry that approach with you into meditation? For example, what's bound to occur if you try to "get peace" through meditation the same way you try to earn the boss's approval at work or to complete a trip to the grocery store in less than an hour? It backfires. That straining, acquisitive attitude is the very opposite of authentic meditation.

Without realizing it, your meditation life can turn into an extension of your daily life. It's a subtle thing, but that's probably the reason many people go through dry spells in which meditation just doesn't seem to work for them anymore.

Watch what can happen if "acquiring peace" has become the goal of meditation just like all the other goals of material life. You sit down for your quiet time, and already you have in mind what you want: peace of mind. It's a commodity, just like a loaf of bread from the store or a larger return on your stock investment. It's something you want and now you're going to use a technique to get it. Concentrating very hard on your mantra or affirmation, you go on the hunt. You're stalking peace. It's hiding somewhere in the fortress of your unconscious. But you think that the power of your focused mind will track it down.

Surely within ten minutes peace will belong to you. Sad to say, after ten, twenty, or even thirty minutes, you're no closer to peace. You get up from your meditation vaguely frustrated and unsatisfied.

So, what *will* work? What's the right approach if you want to experience peace through meditation? The key is *giving* rather than getting. It's a matter of surrendering yourself. Surrendering your worries. Being willing to give up your expectations, and not expecting to get anything— *not even peace.* The whole purpose of this meditation session is *to give.*

Sitting down for your quiet period, you may choose to use a mantra or affirmation. But those words simply help you open your feelings to something bigger than yourself. You're not out to get something; you're *offering* yourself to God. "Here I am. I give up . . . my fears . . . my worries. I surrender . . . my agenda . . . my sense of what's needed."

That basic attitude of turning yourself over to God is the heart of genuine meditation. It's not a technique; it's not a clever maneuver in consciousness. It is simply the offering of oneself. From that surrendering comes a byproduct: the peace of God. What a strange paradox. It's only when you're willing to give up the goal of *acquiring* peace that the *gift* of peace is presented to you.

Mini-motivator: For today's meditation period, take a new approach. Put aside all your expectations about what you might get out of the meditation session. Don't worry about your "performance" as a meditator. For today the whole purpose of those ten or twenty minutes will be surrender. You'll openly offer yourself to God.

Peace Through Self-Knowledge

. . . those that seek to know self may find the way. Those that find the way become content, and find joy, peace . . .   352-1

Something starts to change in late adolescence. A light at the end of the tunnel comes into view. Those middle teenage years have been a confusing mix of emotions and demands.Then, at age seventeen or eighteen, the seed of one's adult self begins to emerge. The quest for self-knowledge begins to bear fruit. Of course, it's a search that will extend into one's twenties and thirties — in fact, it will reach throughout a lifetime. With each step in self-knowledge can come a little more peace of mind and heart.

Teenage life for a girl like Katherine in the 1930s was a lot different than for adolescents in our own times. Those years included the depths of the Depression.

Gender roles were still rigid, and career opportunities for young women were severely limited. Just the same, life in that time wasn't as complex as it is now, and there weren't as many distractions and temptations.

But if we put aside all the differences, what remains is a theme of late adolescent life that's as old as humanity itself: the restless search to know oneself and to shape an independent identity for the adult years ahead. Peace of mind doesn't come easily when you're young and trying to find out who you are.

Katherine was fortunate that her family knew about Edgar Cayce and obtained a reading to help her through that transition period. The information she received at age seventeen was a boost to her self-esteem and a challenge for her future. It emphasized her talents, such as her scholastic abilities in French. She had proven herself time and again with her accomplishments at school. Now she'd face a test in the years immediately ahead.

Her life's path would soon come to a fork, Cayce predicted. One way would involve using her considerable skills in self-indulgent, self-serving ways. The alternative meant putting those talents to constructive use by aiding others, even though it would sometimes require sacrifice. Only one way would lead to peace and contentment.

This fork in the road wasn't to be a single moment in Katherine's future. It would be a type of choice she'd face repeatedly. In many of those situations it wouldn't be immediately obvious which way would lead to peace. There wouldn't always be signposts to mark neatly the options. Only from careful self-study would she be able to recognize the way; only through self-knowledge would she be able to see the path to a peaceful life.

Cayce's advice to Katherine was meant

to last a lifetime. *But it's just as applicable to any of us today*—whether we're seventeen, forty-seven, or seventy-seven. If we want to create a peaceful life, there's always one requirement: Know thyself. Without an understanding of ourselves, we'll constantly fall prey to self-deception and the turmoil it always produces. Without a basis of self-understanding, our decisions will be hit-or-miss, creating instability and uncertainty. Peace begins with self-knowledge.

Mini-motivator: Invest fifteen to thirty minutes today doing something that helps you get to know yourself better. For example, your exercise in self-understanding might be to work on interpreting one of your recent dreams. Or it might be trying something new—some activity that has never fit your familiar self-image—and seeing how it makes you feel.

Not As the World Gives Peace

" . . . My peace I give unto thee—not as
the world giveth peace" in the gratifying
. . . or of looking for ease and comfort
irrespective of that it may bring into the
experiences of others . . .   1440-1

How *does* the world give peace? What
did Jesus mean when He contrasted His
kind of peace with the sort that comes from
material life? The biblical account isn't
very explicit. We're left to figure it out for
ourselves—or to turn to insightful inter-
preters such as Cayce.

First, we might well wonder what quali-
fies this man to comment on an enigmatic
teaching of Jesus. Certainly Cayce had no
formal theological training. But the Bible
was the centerpiece of his life. He read it
cover to cover more than sixty times. He
prayed with it, he dreamed about its char-
acters, he taught its principles in Sunday
school for all his adult years. Because it

was so much a part of his conscious and unconscious life, some of his greatest work as a psychic was making the Bible come alive for people.

Here we have the most important passage in the New Testament about peace. "My peace I give unto thee—not as the world giveth peace." (John 14:27) Surely, if we're ever to understand peace from a spiritual angle, we've got to decipher this statement. Why is the mundane sort of peace so much less than the peace of God?

Cayce elaborates for us. Seeming to move for a moment into Jesus' frame of mind, Cayce adds a description of the inferior form of peace—peace as the world gives. It's a kind of self-complacence that puts personal ease and comfort first. In other words, there is a type of peace that allows one person to have it easy while someone else pays the price. That lucky one who gets the benefit is more likely than not quite willing to stay ignorant of what's really happening.

This very idea is sure to make many of us anxious. If we're members of the privileged class in society, we've probably come to expect the right to certain comforts. We may say to ourselves, "I work hard and I deserve what I've got." But *sometimes* the ease that makes our lives feel a little more peaceful comes at the expense of someone else.

This is hard to accept and face. For example, those of us in the Western world, especially in America, consume a vastly disproportionate share of the earth's resources. Even *within our own country* millions of people go to bed each night hungry and/or inadequately sheltered. If it's too overwhelming to think about such problems on this big a scale, perhaps you can still find examples in the smaller circle of your own family and community. Are there times when you get comfortable benefits at the expense of someone else?

This is a part of Cayce's message about peace that can distress us. Sometimes we'd probably prefer his philosophy to stay focused on metaphysics and abstract universal law. We begin to squirm a little when the readings start talking about being our brother's and sister's keeper. The social and moral dimensions of Cayce's philosophy have all too often been ignored.

But this is an unavoidable part of genuine peace. Cayce asks us to believe that Jesus was calling us to a radical re-evaluation of how we go about our lives. It suggests that there's a superficial kind of peace that comes from comfort and ease. It's actually a bogus form of peace—a caricature of what peace can really be. What makes it an illusory peace? It's *not* so much that the comforts of the world are wrong—the problem is when they come at the expense of others. In those cases, something deep in our souls knows it's not fair. Consciously we may be relaxed and pleased with ourselves, but at our core there's a restless knowing that something's not right.

So what do we do? Feeling guilty about eating a good dinner tonight isn't the answer. Nor is any other form of guilt. What's called for is a willingness to be aware. That sounds simple, but it's not easy. It's a brave person who is able to see how *some* of his or her comforts might be linked to a burden for someone else. It takes courage to recognize how we occasionally settle for the lesser form of peace even though it brings no peace to our souls.

Mini-motivator: Take a careful look at what makes your life easy and comfortable. Try to see how you get a superficial peace of mind or body at the expense of someone else. Simply coming to that awareness is the biggest step. Next, do something—even just a little something at first—that would ease that burden.

The Will to Peace

... peace ... comes from making *thy* will
one with the Creative Forces—which is
love!   1792-2

The world was moving toward war. It
was 1939 and events in Europe were growing more ominous every month. The ter-
rible war that was coming would surely be
a test of wills, but it would also be a test of
machines and technology.

Joseph was one of a handful of scien-
tists and engineers whose secret work
would eventually turn the course of that
war. He would become a key member of the
Manhattan Project team that would create
the first atomic bomb.

But in 1939 it was hard for him to see
the significant role in human history he
would play. Joseph was discouraged and
his self-esteem was sagging. When he wrote
to Cayce and asked for a reading, he was
hoping for something that would lift his

spirits and get his life refocused in a meaningful way.

It is, perhaps, ironic that one of the most succinct statements about peace in all the Cayce readings was given to this man, one of the builders of the atomic bomb. In fact, the statement was preceded by a warning because Cayce described previous lives in which his scientific and engineering skills had been put to the test. More than once before his soul had faced the question of using scientific abilities for either good or evil.

However, the reading didn't threaten Joseph, or give him any ultimatums or try to intimidate him to quit his job. Instead, it talked of peace and of finding peace in his own life.

Peace is essentially an act of your will, the reading told him. It comes from a willingness to let love guide your life. Peace requires an act of will that surrenders — not out of discouragement and defeat —

but out of the knowledge that there's a better way than your own automatic tendencies. Peace means allowing something bigger than yourself to work through you. It means letting go of your own agenda.

Think about what this message for Joseph also means to *you*. If peace is linked to your will, then it gradually emerges from the little choices that you make every day. It's a matter of the small decisions—the ones that could happen almost impulsively, if you're not careful. When you feel a dispute bubbling up with a colleague, do you push willfully for your own way? Or do you let go and invite love to be a guide? If you're not careful and attentive enough, things could move fast and before you know it the contentious bickering has begun.

If you've just been disappointed by a friend and you feel ready to lash out in resentment, what do you do with your will? There's always the possibility of putting your hurt feelings in perspective and letting love direct you. That's when peace happens.

Mini-motivator: Spend a day carefully paying attention to the little choices that you make. Notice when you have an option between pushing for your own way *or* letting go and allowing love to guide the situation. Choose love that day. Decide to willingly allow something bigger than your normal reactions to be in charge. Be an agent of peace.

Spreading Peace

Such peace as the world, or the rabble,
knoweth not . . . every thought, every act,
becomes a *song* in the heart . . .   272-7

By now it seemed too late to turn back.
Theresa's marriage had been going down-
hill for years and now it was at a breaking
point. Her husband Bennett was seemingly too busy with his fast-paced, lucra-
tive career as an attorney. He complained
that he just didn't have the time and
energy for the sort of marriage she wanted.

It wasn't going to be the end of the world
for her. She had her own career as a sixth-
grade teacher. It would mean a step-down
in her style of living since she couldn't
afford to maintain their expensive home on
her salary alone. But she knew that she'd
make do in a more modest setting.

Most of all she wanted to make sure that
this next phase of her life—the post-di-
vorce period—went in the right direction.

So she wrote to her friend Edgar Cayce. She'd known about him for many years, having first heard about his readings in a college classroom. She had received readings on six previous occasions in years past. In fact, Theresa had become a supporter of his work, sending contributions when she heard that finances were tight.

What would this longtime friend and source of sound advice tell her? First, her reading assured her that parting ways with her husband was best. She had tried everything she could do, and now it was time to move on with her life.

Then, as she had found in her previous readings from Cayce, there was an inspiring message of hope. In explicit terms the reading described her spiritual calling in life. She could be a builder of peace in her world. She had a knack for spreading peace. To do so she would have to resist the temptation to go to either of two extremes. One was trying to make a big name in the world—to be someone of notoriety who would influence people in a dramatic way. The other extreme was to withdraw from the world and try to bring peace by quiet solitude. She was warned against these two detours with the words: "Not any great revelation, not in the fanfare of trumpet, not in segregating self from the world . . . " (272-7)

Her life's mission as an agent of peace was to take a middle road. Her gift was in meeting the everyday challenges with a song in her heart. Her special talent was helping people see how troubles and difficulties could be met with *a lightness of spirit*. Because she was innately so good at doing that, her influence would easily transfer from one person to the next. One individual whose troubled mind was made more peaceful by Theresa would naturally do the same for someone else. Like a chain reaction, dozens of people everyday would experience more peace.

Even though this was Theresa's special

gift, to some degree we're all capable of triggering chain reactions of peace. Every day we impact other people—for better *or* for worse—and the influence we impart gets passed on. If we set our minds to it, we can confront difficult situations with songs in our hearts and spread peace wherever we go.

Mini-motivator: The next time a problem comes up in relationship to other people, meet that event with a lightness of spirit. Be a trigger for peace. Feel how your positive attitude is going to have an effect indirectly on many other people today as a peaceful chain reaction is set in motion.

Meeting Christ

Though ye wander far afield, call upon the Lord while He may be found and He will draw very nigh unto thee; and with His presence bring peace.   294-174

The atmosphere was sometimes tense in the Cayce household. The demands on everyone's time and energy were extraordinary. Money was usually in short supply, and small tensions and jealousies surfaced from time to time among the supporters who tried to help Edgar Cayce. On occasion those difficulties would culminate in a major setback, such as the bickering that led to the collapse of the Cayce Hospital in 1928 and the failure of Atlantic University in 1930.

But on other occasions the tension was more subtle, like an undercurrent of frustration. In April of 1934, Cayce himself arranged for a reading about the situation. He knew it was time to get back on track.

Little squabbles and misunderstandings were diverting attention from the real work at hand.

The message offered from his superconscious mind spoke of peace—the most profound kind of peace that humanity could experience. The Christ was at hand. If Cayce and his immediate followers would be alert to experience that Presence, the entire situation would be dramatically transformed.

Of course, it wasn't to himself alone that Cayce offered this sort of advice about finding peace. For example, just one month later he went to great lengths to help a despondent fifty-seven-year-old man who was threatening to commit suicide. On two successive days, Cayce gave readings for this individual, trying to instill the peace of Christ in him.

It was during the second reading for that man that Cayce had a direct encounter with Christ. In fact, on some rare occasions while he gave a reading, another aspect of his mind would independently have dream-like experiences. When these happened, he would regain normal consciousness, not remembering anything he had said in the reading but vividly aware of a simultaneous dream-like experience he had just had.

On that day in mid-May, Cayce's wife Gertrude gave the suggestion for him to awaken following the reading for this suicidal man. But instead, from the entranced state Cayce continued to speak. It had been just a month since that reading for himself had advised his being alert for direct encounters with Christ. Now as he spoke, it was happening. "Jesus of Nazareth passeth by. Let Him fill thine heart with the hopes of those promises that are indeed thine, wilt thou but apply. Trust ye in the Lord." (378-41)

Then Cayce awakened. Although he recalled nothing of what he had just said in the reading—about the troubled man or about Jesus—he told Gertrude of a powerful dream that had just come to him. "I saw the Master walking down a road toward us—*all* of us, expectant, waiting for Him to come—and He was smiling: seemed very happy."

The same promise is ours. The greatest peace imaginable comes from feeling the Presence of Christ. Do we believe it's possible? Maybe what stands in the way is our own limited idea of *how* Christ can draw close to us. We need to expand the possibilities and realize that it's not always a vision or a voice. That Presence may simply come as a feeling—a gentle reminder that we are loved. Or it may come to us as an inner knowing that everything is being worked out according to a plan. We can expand our expectations and let Christ come directly into our experience in a way that uniquely fits our own needs and backgrounds.

Mini-motivator: Dedicate this day for openness to experience directly the peace of Christ. But let go of any preconceived notions of how it may come. Simply be alert and receptive.

Affirmative Approaches
to Peace

. . . such activities and attitudes will
bring into thy experience the greater peace.
Not by "Don't do this—Don't do that! . . . "

528-16

"I'd be at peace if only I didn't have
to . . . " How often do you feel that way,
finishing the sentence with some annoying
responsibility or irksome person you'd like
to eliminate from your life? How frequently
does peace of mind seem only a step away—
a step that draws the line and cuts something out of your life?

It's natural to think of peace in negative
terms. It's a human tendency to expect
peace as the consequence of getting rid of
something. An insensitive neighbor. A
chronic illness. A financial problem. These
are all good candidates for a negative formula for peace, the sorts of items we
assume to be obstacles to peace. Hence,

getting rid of them sounds as if it would probably do the trick.

But that sort of formula is what Cayce sometimes warned against. Searching for peace with a negative approach invites disappointment. Why? Because there is no guarantee that when the trouble is removed peace will be left in its place.

That was Karen's problem. She was caught in a mistaken plan for making her life more peaceful. Certainly there were troubles. Foremost was her health crisis. For two years she had struggled with a painful debilitating skin disease called scleroderma. Sometimes it left her incapable of performing her job as a church organist and choir director.

Perhaps even more painful was her relationship with Jonathan. Several years earlier he had wanted to marry her, but she put him off, not sure that he was really the one for her. She expected him to wait on her, to give her some time to make up her mind. Then her skin disease came along, and the tentative quality of their relationship faded away. He began to date others, especially one younger, attractive woman. Now Karen wanted him. She was sure that Jonathan was the right man for her.

By the time Karen received a reading from Cayce her life was in turmoil. His advice covered both physical—recommendations and remedies for her skin problem—and spiritual aspects. Essentially she needed to find peace. But her method of finding it was really a negative approach: If only I could get rid of this scleroderma, then I'd be peaceful; if only that rival woman would disappear, then my life would be tranquil.

The best formula for her would be the same for you, in whatever troubling condition you find yourself. It involves taking a positive, affirming approach to the search for peace. Temporarily assume that *at*

least for awhile nothing is going to go away.
Now, how will you build peace in your life
in spite of those difficulties? What kind of
steps can you take to create peace in your
experience? Your answer to those questions points the way to peace.

Mini-motivator: Notice where in your
life you've been trying to get rid of something in order to be more peaceful and
content. For a few days suspend that effort. Operate under the assumption that at
least for a time conditions aren't going to
change. Nothing is going to go away.

Now, take some creative, positive steps
to build peace in your life. Replace the
negative approach to peace with an affir-
mative one.

Empathy

... put self in the other fellow's place
... Then may the life be the more joyous,
the more at peace, the more in accord.

930-1

It had been another tormenting night;
three times this week Doug hadn't slept
well. He knew why. It was all the problems
he'd been having with his suppliers. They
weren't coming through on time with the
materials they had promised. As plant
manager, Doug was responsible for doing
something about it.

But why this week? He'd been in management roles with this company for fifteen years. Problems and difficult decisions were part of the job. Yet he couldn't
remember having had his sleep so dis-
turbed in the past. Was it because he had
taken such a tough stance with one of the
tardy suppliers? He had angrily let that
man know that their contract was voided

because of the delay. Sure, he knew this would get the supplier stirred up. But why was Doug's peace of mind eroded by simply following hard-nosed business rules?

The next day over lunch he confided in his friend and fellow businessman Dave Kahn. It was a bit embarrassing to admit that he was losing sleep over something like this, but Dave was a thoughtful man who might have some good advice. Nothing would have prepared Doug for his recommendation: a business consultation from a psychic living 400 miles away. The whole process could be done through the mail, and Doug wouldn't even have to meet this man Edgar Cayce. Even though it sounded strange, he was ready to try anything to regain his peace of mind and to rest at night.

Two weeks later the materials from Cayce arrived. Four typed pages that analyzed Doug's character and business life. At first he was skeptical. Dave must have tipped

Cayce off because no one could know some of this information. But as he thought more carefully, he realized that not even his friend Dave knew some of these facts about his feelings and hopes.

Cayce's most important piece of business advice focused on empathy. Doug already had the management skills to do well at his job, it stated. The only question was whether or not he had the people skills to find peace and contentment in his profession. The secret was getting inside the thinking and life experience of someone else. " . . . put self in the other fellow's place." (930-1) Then Doug would be able to see what needed to be done. Sometimes it would require being tough and hard-nosed. Other times it might mean being a little more patient and tolerant. Each situation would be different, and no management book could provide firm guidelines.

Doug was going to have to learn this new skill: being empathic. Cayce promised

him a good night's sleep. He'd rest well
after any day that he practiced a willingness to look at situations from the other
person's point of view. Peace of mind and
peace of heart were within his reach. But
he was going to have to make some changes.

Mini-motivator: Every time today that
you encounter a situation that upsets your
peace of mind, try being empathic. Use
your imagination to re-create the events
from the point of view of the other person.
How do you suppose he or she has experienced what's been happening? After you've
done this, act on what seems fair and right
for everyone involved.

Right Effort

Know in *yourself* that you are doing the right, and let the move be on the part of others . . . the mental satisfaction of knowing that ye are *trying* makes a peace that may not be had otherwise.   1183-3

None of us can make someone else change. But when we're in a disruptive situation that destroys our peace, we know we've got to do *something*. Janet was in one of the worst situations imaginable. Her husband was alcoholic and dependent. What made matters even worse, the lady she had taken in as a boarder was irritable and disturbing. These two people were making her life miserable, and she developed a bad case of high blood pressure.

Janet sought help from Cayce for two reasons. She knew she needed to control her hypertension. Otherwise, it might leave her vulnerable to a stroke. She realized that something had to change in her chaotic, tense home life.

Her reading from Cayce promised her the peace that she wanted so desperately. It would require that she follow a careful strategy for dealing with these issues. First, the disruptive renter had to go; she wasn't likely to change her ways. The news could be broken lovingly to the woman, but Janet had to be firm in her resolve.

The problem with her husband wouldn't be so easily handled. According to Cayce, the alcoholism was in a very advanced and serious stage. Although there was still a chance that he would get hold of his life and change, there were no guarantees. In such an impossible situation, how could Janet hope to find peace of mind? Cayce proposed a formula to her.

His recommendation goes right to the heart of human psychology. It contains advice that any of us could apply if we found ourselves in a seemingly hopeless tangle with someone. Resist the temptation to think that it's all up to you. Make peace with yourself by doing *everything* you can to help the situation — but then let go of any expectations about how conditions will turn out. If you know that you've done your very best, then it won't be hard to find an inner peace, even if situations around you are still in turmoil.

Continuing this line of reasoning, Cayce told Janet to watch her words and deeds carefully. Never do anything for which you might feel regret later. No matter what others say or do about this unfortunate situation, follow what you know is the best for you. If you're successful at this, the peace that has been promised to you is assured.

It takes great courage to follow that pathway through an emotional upheaval. Our natural human tendency is to blame — sometimes to blame the other person for the unfairness of it all; sometimes to blame ourselves for not being strong enough or

wise enough to make it all turn out right.
But the most reliable way to a genuine
peace is to make sure each day that we've
done our best and then leave the results in
God's hands.

Mini-motivator: Pick one situation in
your life where you've been trying to change
situations and make them better. Try a
new strategy—one that promises to help
you maintain an inner peace. Make a commitment to do your very best in the situation, but let go of the tension that comes
from thinking it's all up to you.

Sustaining World Peace

For what preserves the equanimity of the earth today? The same as did in that illustration recorded in how Abram or Abraham pled for the cities . . . these have held, these do hold, opportunities open for others.   877-9

Sometimes current events are so upsetting that you probably want to put down the newspaper or turn off the TV evening news. What's keeping the world from completely going down the tubes anyway? It seems as if everything ought to sink from the weight of pain, suffering, and selfishness.

Cayce's answer to this troubling question was to recall the Old Testament story of Abraham. Although God was ready to destroy Sodom because of its corruption, He entered into a bargain with Abraham. If a sufficient number of righteous people could be identified, that would be enough to warrant sparing the city. First the target number was 40 people, but after some negotiating, the figure was lowered to just 10. Unfortunately not even 10 righteous souls could be found.

Assuming that this story describes a spiritual law, just how does it work? How can a small number of people sustain relative peace and stability in the world? By what power is this possible? Is it even fair? It would appear more lawful if every person, community, and nation had to pay for its shortcomings.

Cayce's answers offer an interesting slant on these questions. It's not so much that a handful of people can *save* a city or a country. In fact, no one can override the free will or the destiny of another. If a society is intent on self-destruction, it will probably destroy itself eventually.

What a righteous group *can* do, however, is alter the tone of the situation. It can "hold opportunities open" for everyone. In other words, the consciousness and the actions of a relatively small number of enlightened people have a far-reaching impact. It's not an influence that nullifies the freedom of anyone, but it keeps options from getting closed off; it keeps the alternative for peace and righteousness available.

Sometimes this happens simply by example. Particularly in this day and age of mass media, it's possible for millions of people to know about the inspiring deeds of a small group of committed individuals. That knowledge keeps the possibility open. On other occasions, parapsychology may have the best explanation for how the influence is communicated. If we really are connected to everyone else at a subconscious level—as psychical research suggests—then the high ideals and peace-loving acts of even just a few people have a widespread effect. Through a kind of unconscious telepathy, the option for peace stays alive in every one. Admittedly, for peace to be a reality, it still requires that individuals choose that option. But an extraordinary contribution is made by those who simply keep the "opportunities open for others." (877-9)

Mini-motivator: Be an agent for peace today—peace that extends far beyond your close circle of friends and acquaintances. Try to be aware of your connections to the rest of humanity. Feel how each peaceful thought or deed helps to keep that option available to people all over the world.

Honesty

Be honest with self as you would have others be honest with thee. In that manner ye may overcome all those things that bring doubt or fear.   2509-2

Her life felt as if it were slipping away. The hopeful prospects of a fulfilling career and a happy marriage—possibilities that seemed within reach just a few years earlier—now looked more and more remote. Alice was beginning to be afraid that she might end up alone and embittered.

She was now forty-six. For nine years she had been the social companion of a kind-hearted, supportive man who had come into her life just when she had been deeply disappointed by another man. But her current friend was still married. For more than a decade he had been separated from his wife but had never taken steps to legally break the bond. Although Alice at times had intentions of speaking up and honestly confronting him about this situation, somehow she was never able to be forthright. For that matter, she wasn't even sure that she was being honest with herself or clear about what she really wanted from this relationship.

The problem with truthfulness confronted her in her workplace, too. She was employed on Capitol Hill by a member of the U.S. House of Representatives. She was a top-notch office manager with fourteen years' experience, excellent Washington connections, and the respect of many influential people in government. But for some unexplainable reason, the Congressman for whom she now worked gave her none of the responsibilities and authority she had had when she worked for another Congressman. To make matters worse, he had brought with him to the Capitol the secretary from his own law office who was an ambitious, arrogant, insecure woman. The daily office situation was becoming almost insufferable for Alice. Still she didn't speak up, she didn't honestly express her frustrations.

When she finally turned to Cayce for advice, she wanted to know why she felt misunderstood, fearful, and without any real peace in her life. The reading that came back to her contained one direct message about those problems: the need for greater honesty. If she could be truthful—first to herself and then with others— her fears would dissipate.

Why is honesty so hard for many of us? Sometimes we worry about the reactions that a candid statement will stimulate. Other times we may be embarrassed to admit our genuine feelings. Everybody wrestles to some degree with being frank and open in relationships. Of course, discretion is also important. It's foolish to blurt out everything you think or feel. Timing is critical; so, too, is skill at knowing how to word your statements.

But there's a key to honesty, and it promises to diminish fear and promote inner peace. The secret is to be honest *with oneself first.* That was Alice's mistake. She hadn't found the courage to face herself and honestly recognize what she wanted from her life. Until that happened nothing was going to change in her love relations or in her professional life.

Mini-motivator: Take ten or fifteen minutes for a sincere review of your current life situation. Write down your observations. One by one go through the most significant aspects of your life and be honest with yourself. What are you feeling? What do you want in that relationship or situation? Now start being more honest with others.

Influencing Others

Fear . . . always creates activity in the mind of those feared; but *love* . . . brings harmony or quiet . . .   290-1

He had been gone for four years. Now one day—out of the blue—he appeared at her doorstep. Margaret was flustered. A contradictory mixture of emotions welled up in her: relief, happiness, anger, bitterness. She tried to remain calm as she invited him in.

This was no stranger. Philip was the father of her seven children, and for the first dozen years of their marriage he had been the perfect husband. Then one day without warning he had left Margaret and the family. She had to go to work to support them, eventually becoming quite successful as the owner of her own insurance business. The oldest child, Sandra, had taken over many of the mothering duties.

The entire family had adapted to Philip's absence. Now he was back.

Philip had returned with every intention of staying. Margaret accepted him and tried to put on a normal front for the children and the community as if nothing had happened. But she was only pretending, and after a while her patience wore thin. He had no plans for going back to work himself, apparently assuming that she would support him. Although she didn't complain, she knew this set-up wasn't right.

Finally, after a year of putting up with the awkward arrangement, she knew she needed to find a remedy for this family problem. She thought she knew where she could get some useful advice. A year earlier she had gone with her friend Louise to witness a psychic reading from Edgar Cayce. Louise, seeking help for a physical ailment, had wanted a companion that day of the reading. So Margaret contacted Mr.

Cayce and secured an appointment for her own reading. Louise went along, too, this time as the supportive one herself.

Margaret's most pressing question was whether or not she and her children were in any immediate danger from him. Clearly something was still imbalanced or un-settled in Philip. Was there a chance he would turn violent?

Cayce offered a clairvoyant view of him. His troubled soul needed a reawakening and a renewal. Margaret's attitude and behavior would be pivotal. On the one hand, she should not be condemning but, on the other hand, not pampering nor compliant. Most important of all was her attitude. If she was afraid, it would stir up fear in him. If she continually thought about all that could go wrong, it would only make him more likely to move in that direction.

This sound advice from Cayce reminds us what a strong influence we have on others, particularly family members, relatives, neighbors, and work colleagues. Especially in the case of someone who is vulnerable, our own fears can tip the balance. Troubled or confused individuals are very sensitive to the thoughts and feelings of those around them—often without being directly aware of how easily they are influenced. But this fact can also be used in a positive way. Just as our own fearful thoughts stimulate fear in others, so as much do our loving thoughts make it easier for them to find peace of mind.

Mini-motivator: Pick a person in your life who seems to be going through a difficult time. Make a special effort to keep your thoughts about that individual constructive and life-affirming.

Oneness in the Midst
of Duality

For life and death are one, and only those who will consider the experience as one may come to understand or comprehend what peace indeed means.   1977-1

Physical life is based on duality. Light and dark. Positive- and negative-charged particles of the atom. Male and female gender distinctions. Liberal and conservative political differences. The list goes on and on. In fact, we come to expect polarity in everything we encounter.

Duality gives life its tension. At its best that entails a creative, dynamic interplay that moves us along the path of growth. But more often than not, the tension of duality paralyzes us. Peace is destroyed as we feel pulled apart by competing demands. For example, it's a rare person who would experience peace in trying to reconcile the masculine and feminine aspects of self—whether in love relationships or in the inner alchemy of meeting one's own opposite sex characteristics.

Nowhere, however, is the threat to personal peace more evident than in the most fundamental duality of human existence: *the polarity of life and death*. The stark reality of physical death is an unavoidable matter for all of us. It's an issue for even the most healthy, life-affirming person. Consciously or unconsciously, our peace of mind is eroded by the inevitability of our own impending death.

What's to be done, then, if we want to attain peace in a world of polar opposites? Is peace an unachievable ideal in this world of duality? Perhaps we can bring a *spiritual* understanding to a *physical* law. The physical world, yes, operates by duality. We're also beings of spirit. This reality makes it feasible for us to reconcile and integrate opposites. For example, it's possible to experience oneself as a soul and

harmoniously blend the qualities of masculine and feminine. Even more funda-
mentally, from the spiritual perspective we
can see that earthly life and death are two
sides of the same coin.

Only those who consider life and death
as a oneness will be able to understand
what peace means. That basic principle
came from Cayce in response to the needs
of a New York City jail inmate. In fact,
before giving the reading, Cayce went to
visit the man in prison. He wasn't a hard-
ened killer who was facing the death pen-
alty. He wasn't facing the realities of life
and death any more directly than millions
of people do every day. He was simply a
man who had made some mistakes in a
difficult world where peace is hard to find.

The man was determined to turn his life
around. The district attorney was inclined
to offer him another chance. Cayce's advice in the reading gave him a guiding
principle: Keep looking for the continuity

of life. Try to see the tension-producing dualities from the angle of your spiritual self. Peace will be yours when you can see the underlying oneness.

Mini-motivator: Pick one of the many polar tensions of physical life that may be upsetting your peace of mind. For example, it could be worries about death, troubles in a love relation, or contrary points of view with a work associate. Try for a day to see the issue from the perspective of your spiritual self—a point of view that operates from oneness.

Avoiding Offense

. . . it was necessary that offenses come but that the self should not be offended nor offend others, and with such an attitude one will indeed eventually find peace in self.   3342-1

People who are thin-skinned find it hard to be at peace. Slights, slurs, rudeness — these are the ingredients of fast-paced, tension-filled modern life. Anyone who is quick to take offense will find plenty about which to get upset.

It's not enough that we feel hurt and offended at the time the affront occurs. When we're mistreated, we also tend to hang on to the memory. We keep track of who owes us — a kind of mental ledger in which accounts are kept. The disruption to our peace of mind, therefore, extends for days or weeks afterward.

What can you do personally to minimize this disturbing human trait? How can you learn to avoid taking offense when you're treated badly? The first step is to remember that more often than not the offending party doesn't really have you personally in mind as a target. You haven't been singled out in a premeditated, purposeful way. That individual is unhappy and simply takes it out on the surrounding world. The person wants to share his or her misery, and unfortunately you happened to get in the way. Of course, realizing that you weren't the intended target doesn't erase the annoyance or the trouble. But it can make it a little easier to let go of any resentful memory.

Another strategy is to refuse to take the offense. Just as you can refuse a C.O.D. package or a collect phone call, you can decline the wound it may give to your self-esteem. You may not be able to stop the behavior itself, but you have control over the mood it creates in you. No doubt you've experienced the difference between an irritating action and the subjective feeling of being offended. If a toddler spits up on you, you probably won't like it, but you're not going to feel offended.

It's just one more step to being able to control your own reactions to rude and thoughtless behavior. You don't have to like the way you've been treated—and may even need to communicate firmly your displeasure—but you can choose not to take it as a personal offense that destroys your peace of mind.

In fact, this capacity to rise above hurt feelings has long been recognized as a secret to peace. Apparently it's not just the modern world that's filled with insensitive people. As the Old Testament psalmist put it: "Great peace have those who love thy law, and nothing shall offend them." (Psalm 119:165, King James Version)

Mini-motivator: For one day make this commitment to yourself: I won't take

offense at any mistreatment or slight that
I receive from someone. I don't have to like
everything that comes my way—I may need
to speak up about something—but I won't
let any slight, slur, or annoyance under-
mine my peace.

Creating Peace

Remember, ye pursue peace, ye embrace peace, ye hold to peace. It is not something that descends upon thee, save as ye *have* created and do create it in the hearts, in the minds, in the experiences of others.   3051-2

When we're tired and hassled, we'd love to have peace descend on us like a dove from heaven. It's easy to imagine that sort of magical intervention. Like a troubled child whose parent steps in to save it, peace would simply be there.

The problem is that's not the way life operates. Peace is ours, but we've got to create it—or, perhaps more accurately put, *co-create* it with God. Peace is a byproduct of our efforts. It requires us to take an *active* stance in the world.

In fact, peace is a lot like patience. Both are frequently understood—or misunderstood—to be exclusively a passive relationship with the surrounding world. For example, when we're told to be patient, what's really the message? Be willing to wait. Passively put up with what's going on, and after a while conditions will change.

But to understand fully either patience or peace we need to see its active side, too. Active patience is first of all an inner process, a careful attention to one's attitudes and feelings. For instance, standing in line for an hour without complaining isn't really patience if one is inwardly stewing with frustration. But, of course, active patience also has an outer element. The truly patient person doesn't merely sit back and wait for changes to happen. That individual gets involved and works unhurriedly for something new.

So what would *active peace* look like? First, it's an attitude, a recognition that harmony won't supernaturally materialize all by itself. We're going to have to *do something* to help them come forth.

Second, it's a willingness to get involved in the lives of others in a purposeful way. There's a *social dimension* to active peace. As we help others to experience peace in their own lives, it comes alive in our own as well. To many people this is a rather radical idea. The more familiar image of peace entails getting away from people — finding some peace and quiet by oneself. Even though there's certainly a need for times alone, the idea of active peace turns the conventional theory upside down — it claims there's another side to the story. Instead of passivity, it means activity. Rather than separation, it encourages involvement. Maybe up until now we've been looking for peace with only half the picture in mind.

Mini-motivator: Take an active stance today for peace. Look for situations in which you can take steps to build peace, especially for opportunities to help other people experience it.

Children of Peace

And if you commit that peace to thy son,
he—too—may put his hand in the hand of
the Master . . .   3165-1

These words from Edgar Cayce had a
powerful effect on Carolyn. For several
years she had been increasingly concerned
about her son Jeffrey. He seemed to be an
overly sensitive child, with a slight stam-
mer and a problem with bed-wetting. He
was overly attached to her, constantly
clinging to her, and seemed unable to
enjoy being with other people. In so many
ways he appeared to be underdeveloped,
as if he were eight or nine years old instead
of his real age, eleven.

Carolyn worried that she was the cause
of these difficulties. While she was pregnant with him, many situations in her life
made her extremely unhappy. Could her
depression have been transmitted to Jeffrey in such a way that his development

was retarded slightly? Or was it something she was doing *now* that was continuing to contribute to the problem?

Cayce's reading was for Jeffrey, but many of the comments and suggestions were directed toward Carolyn. He confirmed that Jeffrey was born with certain emotional disturbances and that his mother's emotional state had had an impact. But all that was in the past. There was no use in feeling guilty when many positive things could be done right now to assist him.

First, Cayce recommended that Carolyn adopt greater peace of mind about his slow development. He would catch up. In their own timing, the changes would come naturally.

Next, the reading described the kind of parental support that would help Jeffrey experience greater peace and security himself. Just as Carolyn's prenatal emotions influenced her son, even eleven years later there was still a connection. If she would clarify her own ideals and beliefs, it would subtly affect him. If she would focus and commit her energies to high values and purposes, it would boost Jeffrey's ability to start doing the same for his own life. Most of all, Carolyn could be an influence for peace in the life of her son. In doing so, it would enable him, as he grew older, to build a stronger and stronger relationship to Christ.

Teaching peace to our children is a potent message. We live in a world that continually bemoans the academic skills of our youth, that criticizes their social habits, and worries about their lack of commitment to high values. But what have we taught them about peace? Rather than blame teachers, television, or video games, we'd do better to examine our own influence on them. We all have children in our lives—whether we're parents, grandparents, aunts, uncles, or next-door neighbors. We all have a responsibility to teach peace to the younger generation.

Mini-motivator: Make a focused effort to be a teacher of peace to one child in your life. First of all, by your example demonstrate what living peacefully looks like. In addition, try to find ways that you can promote peace of mind for that child, as well as peaceful relationships with friends and family.

Opposing Fear

For fear is — as it ever has been — that
influence that opposes will, and yet fear is
only of the moment while will is of eternity.

1210-1

Ted had worked hard to become successful in his career as a physician — college, medical school, and then years gain-
ing his reputation as a first-class doctor.
But when he reached his early 50s, everything started to change. He lost interest in
medicine and quit, and his marriage began
to come apart. It was at that point that a
friend in New York told him about Cayce,
and Ted decided to request a reading about
his life's purpose.

"Should I go back to medical practice?"
he asked. Not full time, was Cayce's advice. You need more freedom in your life's
path. In fact, freedom is the key to understanding your mission in this lifetime.

The reading told a detailed story of his

soul's purpose—for this current lifetime *and* for the preceding one in which he had also worked as a physician. During the Revolutionary War he "looked after the health as related to cleanliness about the encampments . . . " (1210-1) But his constant goal was more than preventing infections and healing wounds. It was also freedom. This meant the cause of the colonists fighting British oppression; and it also meant *freedom from fear.*

So strong was this commitment that it carried over into his 20th-century lifetime. He had come with powerful urges to promote freedom, especially to help other people break loose from anything that would bind them. In particular, his calling was to assist individuals to be free of their fears. Cayce even summarized this mission for Ted in a succinct statement of his soul's purpose: " . . . to *free souls* from fear!" (1210-1)

That's a noble undertaking. How does

one do it? How do we get rid of our own
fears, let alone help someone else do it?
Cayce's recommendations to this fifty-four-
year-old man included one important clue:
Awaken your free will. Recognize that any
fear is the opposite of will—it is the antith-
esis of freedom. If you've surrendered your
will and you're letting other people or out-
side events control your life, then you're
bound to be fearful.

That clue can lead us to a remarkable
discovery: Something extraordinary happens when we use free will and *act*, even in
the face of fear. By doing something—
rather than being paralyzed—our sense of
time is altered. What dawns on us is that
fear is only momentary—the situation or
person that scares us is temporary. But
something else is timeless. That other in-
gredient that comes clearly into focus is
the will—that is, our freedom and our
individuality. We experience our own time-
lessness and our own place in eternity.

Mini-motivator: The next time you're anxious or afraid, use this affirmation: "This fear is only momentary—my real self is eternal." Use the words to help you get in touch with the continuity of life, your own immortality. Then *act* in the situation. Do something—the best that you know to do. Use your will, knowing that free will is the opposite of fear.